Kinds of Fruits

by Sara E. Hoffmann

first step nonfiction

Lerner Publications Company · Minneapolis

Apples grow.

Grapes grow.

Oranges grow.

Cherries grow.

All of these are fruits.

Fruits grow!

The images in this book are used with the permission of: © Galina Ermolaeva/Dreamstime .com, p. 2; © Daniela Pelazza/Shutterstock.com, p. 3; © Arkady/Shutterstock.com, p. 4; © Fotokostic/Shutterstock.com, p. 5; © atoss/Shutterstock.com, p. 6 (orange); © aarows/ Shutterstock.com, p. 6 (grapes); © Denny Smythe/Dreamstime.com, p. 6 (apple); © Ahi/ Dreamstime.com, p. 6 (cherries); © Angelo Gilardelli/Dreamstime.com, p. 7.

Front cover: © sarsmis/Shutterstock.com.

Main body text set in ITC Avant Garde Gothic Std Medium 21/25.
Typeface provided by Adobe Systems.

Lerner Publications Company
A division of Lerner Publishing Group, Inc.
241 First Avenue North
Minneapolis, MN 55401 U.S.A.

Website address: www.lernerbooks.com

Library of Congress Cataloging-in-Publication Data

Hoffmann, Sara E.
    Kinds of fruits / by Sara E. Hoffmann.
        p.   cm. — (First Step Nonfiction—Kinds of plants)
    ISBN 978–1–4677–0491–5 (pbk. : alk. paper)
    1. Fruit—Juvenile literature. I. Title.
QK660.H64 2013
634—dc23   2012002932

Manufactured in the United States of America
1 – BP – 7/15/12

Expand learning beyond the printed book. Download free, complementary educational resources for this book from our website, www.lernerresource.com.